Instant Pot Cookbook for Vegetarians

Electric Pressure Cooker Guide Through Best Selected Goodies Ever

ALEXANDER BOUCHARD

Table of Contents

Introduction

I want to thank you and congratulate you for purchasing the book, *"Instant Pot Cookbook for Vegetarians: Electric Pressure Cooker Guide Through Best Selected Goodies Ever"*.

This book contains proven steps and strategies on how to use your Instant Pot or some other electric pressure cooker to make all kinds of meals. Not only that, the book teaches you how to make delicious, yet healthy meals without spending hours in the kitchen.

Hectic lifestyle doesn't allow us to spend too much time in the kitchen making homemade meals. When you come home from work, the last thing you want is to stand behind the stove and wait for your dinner to be ready.

With Instant Pot and other electric pressure cookers, you have the opportunity to cook and prepare your meal in less than 30 minutes. Throughout the pages of this book, you will find useful information about pressure cooking and Instant Pots as well as myths you should stop believing.

Not only that, the book also features multiple recipes for breakfast, lunch, dinner, desserts, soups, and so much more. The cookbook doesn't stop there, it shows you don't need to have some advanced, MasterChef-like cooking skills to make delicious meals. As a result, you'll feel motivated to cook more and create your own dishes.

If you have ever wanted to try delicious, fast, and healthy meals, then you'll love this book. Recipes found here are so tasty even omnivores would want to eat them all the time.

This book is suitable for vegetarians, vegans, busy students, parents, working people, as well as for readers who aren't vegetarians, but want to have a healthier lifestyle. Regardless of who you are, you'll relate to the content of this book.

Without a further ado, let's step into the world of a healthy and convenient approach to cooking. Amazingly delicious meals are just a few taps away.

Thanks again for buying this book, I hope you enjoy it!

Chapter 1: 6 Things You Should Know about Your Instant Pot

You just bought your very first instant pot? Or maybe you are still thinking about purchasing one? Being a beginner in this whole new way of cooking or thinking about dipping your toes in these water always comes with a dose of nervousness.

At this point, you don't know if pressure cooking is the right option for you or how you would handle it. Don't feel bad; these feelings are entirely natural.

All those articles from unreliable sources don't make it easier for you to adopt pressure cooking. They make it seem so complicated, right?

One thing you should know is that you don't really need some exceptional culinary skills to use a pressure cooker. This appliance is incredibly easy to use and as you use it more often, your experience and cooking skills will develop.

I'm going to start this book with a basic rundown of things that every new pressure cooker owner and people who are still debating whether to get this appliance should know.

1. It is intuitive

What does this mean? If you've never used any type of pressure cooker before, it will take some time for you to get used to the new cooking style. At the same time, it's not complicated to learn everything about it.

This is not a bad thing!

Instant Pot comes with various settings and buttons to consider. Read the manual from top to bottom before you even start thinking about meals to make.

It's even better to write down basic instructions and buttons on a piece of paper and keep it in your kitchen so you don't look for the manual all the time.

Ideally, you should start with simple recipes first, before you move on to more complex meals. Throughout this book, you'll find recipes with different levels of difficulties.

2. Pressure-can, no you can't!

One of the most common questions about the Instant Pot is whether you can use pressure-can.

The answer is: no, you cannot!

Why?

A Pressure sensor regulates pressure cooker, not a thermometer. As a result, the actual temperature might change depending on your location's elevation. Moreover, the USDA did not test the safety of Instant Pot in pressure-canning.

On the other hand, you can do boiling-water canning which is suitable for jams and pickles.

3. Instant Pots are easy to clean

If you are tired of all those appliances that are difficult to clean, you will love your Instant Pot.

Instant Pot has a multitude of advantages, but one of the best things about it is a simple and easy cleaning process.

Not only is it going to help you save some space in your kitchen, but you won't waste your time on cleaning the unit. Basically, the process is:

- Unplug the appliance (of course!)

- Wipe exterior of housing to remove tough stains and crumbs

- Using a small brush remove dried food in the recessed area of the unit

- Hand-wash the lid with soapy, warm water

- Remove the steam release handle and anti-block shield, sealing ring, and float valve

- Wash the inner pot and steam rack

- Wipe or soak with vinegar in order to remove the well-known rainbowing effect or discolorations on the stainless steel

- Reassemble

4. You'll have to convert 15 psi recipes

The reason for this is simple – pressure cookers operate at 15 psi, 250°F, (pounds per square inch) while the Instant Pot functions at 11.6 psi or 242°F.

Therefore, when you come across recipes which recommend 15psi, the best thing to do is to cook a few minutes longer.

5. *Sauté feature can do way more*

Sauté is just one of many features that come with your Instant Pot, and it's safe to say it will be one of your favorite options to use.

Why?

That's because it is quite versatile. You can:

- Sauté vegetables before cooking a meal in order to soften them up and enhance the flavor of the dish

- Cook pasta e.g. when you are about to prepare a soup which includes pasta. After the cooking cycle is done and depressurized, you can proceed to open your Instant Pot and hit the sauté option. In a few minutes, it will start boiling. Once it does, you just have to add pasta and cook for about 10 minutes or so. Chicken noodle soup tastes divine this way

- Thicken sauces by mixing cornstarch with cold water and adding the mixture to a sauce in the pot. Then, turn on the sauté and wait for a few minutes

- Make a roux to enhance the flavor of your meal just by sautéing flour and oil until the mixture gets the color of peanut butter

6. *Research, research, research*

This is for people who still didn't purchase their instant pot, but they want to own one in order to make lovely and healthy vegetarian meals.

Even though the Instant Pot is its own brand, many other manufacturers offer pressure cookers with similar characteristics. Before you make the purchase, don't be afraid to research all those brands e.g. Breville, Cuisinart, Gournmia.

Get informed about the characteristics of their products. Then, opt for the one that suits you and your needs or preferences better than other options on the market.

Chapter 2: Difference between Electric and Stove-Top Pressure Cookers

Pressure cooking is highly practical and it has become a popular cooking method. We can divide pressure cookers into electric and stove-top appliances.

While it is easy to assume these units are the same, they do have a lot of differences and this chapter is going to uncover them.

Electric vs. stove-top pressure cookers

Generally speaking, electric cookers are easier to use for most people while stove-top pressure cookers are usually suitable for individuals with advanced cooking skills.

Electric pressure cookers are ideal for people who are nervous about setting heat settings. These appliances do it automatically and you, pretty much, have nothing to worry about.

If you are swamped with appliances of all kinds including rice cooker, yogurt maker, or slow cooker, you can give them away or donate because electric pressure cooker can replace them all. Basically, these units are more versatile.

A major advantage of electric pressure cookers over stove-top appliances is that they are perfect for users who don't have too much time on their hands. Seniors, students, busy parents, regardless of your age or occupation, these appliances are proper time-savers.

Comparison

To truly understand the difference between electric pressure cookers and stove-top appliances, you need to see how they compare to one another.

- While stove-top units have 2 or more pressure settings, electric cookers feature a more varied maximum pressure

- When using a stove-top pressure cooker, you are the one who adjusts the heat. On the other hand, electric units do it automatically

- A vast majority of stove-top appliances don't have an integrated timer while all electric pressure cookers do

- Even though electric cookers do have a longer release time than stove-top appliances, the thermos-like construction improves the efficiency of the unit by keeping the heat from the coil inside the cooker instead of dissipating it all over your kitchen

Advantages of electric pressure cookers

Although it is easy to assume electric and stove-top cookers are almost the same, they have multiple differences (as shown above).

If you're wondering whether you made a right choice by opting for Instant Pot or some similar pressure cooker, the benefits listed below will prove you made a great decision.

Benefits of electric pressure cookers include:

- 5-in-1 kitchen unit

- 8 one-key operation buttons for the most frequent cooking tasks

- Convenience

- Delayed cooking option to allow you to plan the meal ahead of time

- Designed to avoid or eliminate potential safety problems

- Fully insulated housing thus reducing the energy being dispersed without cooking the food to a bare minimum

- Integrated heat source that creates a full feedback system which regulates the cooking cycle

- Programmable electric control capability

Instant Pot and similar appliances pose as the future of healthy and convenient cooking. When it comes to the convenience, Instant Pot is an absolute winner.

With a multitude of options, features, and settings, electric pressure cookers are more practical for people who are on the go. Yes, you made a wonderful choice by purchasing Instant Pot or some other electric pressure cooker.

As a vegetarian, you are looking for different ways to make your meals while retaining the benefits of the ingredients and the Instant Pot is an ideal solution for your needs.

Chapter 3: Doesn't Pressure Cooking Kill Nutrients in Food?

Wait, but is pressure cooking healthy? After all, this cooking style kills all the important nutrients!

Let's be honest, you've probably thought this same thing. We all did at some point or another. In fact, this is one of the most common myths about pressure cooking.

Yes, I used the word *myth* on purpose, because that's just what it is – a myth. Pressure cooking does NOT kill all the nutrients and it is incredibly healthy.

Before you start preparing wonderful vegetarian meals, it is important to clarify this enormous misconception that prevents a lot of people from using their electric pressure cooker regularly.

Vitamins and minerals are NOT destroyed

Pressure cookers, regardless of the type, destroy vitamins and minerals. That's a common belief, but the reality is entirely different.

You will be surprised to know that more vitamins and minerals are retained through pressure cooking than with other cooking methods such as steaming or boiling.

The process saves and reuses the cooking liquid, thus providing the maximum vitamin/mineral retention.

For example, a study whose findings were published in the Journal of *Food Science* evaluated retention of vitamin C in broccoli using five cooking techniques. Scientists discovered that steaming and boiling led to major vitamin C losses (22% and 34%

19

respectively) while other cooking methods (pressure-cooking, microwaving) retained more than 90% of the vitamin C content[1].

As you can see, pressure cooking doesn't kill the nutrients in food, it preserves them. In turn, you get much-needed vitamins, minerals, antioxidants, other compounds that your body requires in order to function properly and remain healthy.

No carcinogens

Some cooking methods, such as grilling or frying, produce carcinogens that could jeopardize your health. Pressure cooking is different!

Unlike other high-heat cooking methods, pressure cooking doesn't produce carcinogenic compounds like *acrylamide.*

It is important to mention that starchy foods are usually the ones that develop carcinogenic compounds when handled at temperatures above 248°F.

Even though Instant Pot and similar appliances can go even higher than this temperature, they still don't produce carcinogens due to the moist environment.

A group of researchers discovered that compared to other high-temperature cooking methods, 20 minutes of pressure cooking did not induce the formation of acrylamides in potatoes[2].

---

[1] Galgano F, Favati F, Caruso M, et al. The influence of processing and preservation on the retention of health-promoting compounds in broccoli. *Journal of Food Science*, January 29, 2007, 72: S130-S135. Doi: 10.1111/j.1750-3841.2006.00258.x

[2] Patents: Method for reducing acrylamide formation in thermally processed foods. US 8114463 B2

Now, if we bear in mind that you need only 10 minutes only to cook potatoes in your Instant Pot, it means you're entirely safe.

Health benefits of pressure cooking

Compared to other popular methods, pressure cooking is safe and healthy. Even science confirmed the advantages of pressure cookers, thus debunking those common myths that are circling around.

Now that we have established pressure cooking is healthy, here are some important health benefits you should know about these units:

- Nutrient retention

- Healthy meals are prepared fast

- Decreased intake of fats and calories

- Reduced risk of consumption of foodborne pathogens

- Improved food digestibility

- Regular digestion

- Weight management

Chapter 4: Tips to Bear in Mind and Mistakes to Avoid

You're very close to starting your Instant Pot adventure with delicious and healthy meals and yummy desserts. Before you do so, there are some things you should know or mistakes to avoid. This chapter brings you a few pointers that will only enhance your electric pressure cooker experience.

Tips

- Cooking time mentioned in the recipe is not, actually, the total amount of time it will take for your unit to finish cooking. But, how? Well, Instant Pot needs a few minutes to heat up in order to begin cooking, and it also needs a few minutes to release. Generally, the total cooking time is about 10 minutes longer than written in a recipe, depending on your appliance of course

- Want to prepare a meal using frozen vegetables? Or maybe you want to make a dessert with frozen fruits? Regardless of your intention, it is not necessary to thaw frozen fruits or veggies before cooking in an electric pressure cooker

- Instant Pot allows you to use dried beans and grains without soaking them first. Yet another example that shows how Instant pot saves time

- Before you add dry grains and legumes to the pot, you do need to rinse them first, of course

- Instant Pot allows you to cook foods in glass jars as long as they are smaller than the bowl

- You can take out the sealing ring to clean or replace it. A common complaint among Instant Pot users is the odd smell coming out of the sealing ring, without being aware they can remove this part easily and clean it first or replace it after some time

- Make sure the pressure value is set to *sealing* instead of *venting* when you're about to make your meal. Otherwise, the unit wouldn't be able to come to pressure

Mistakes to avoid

- Forgetting to place the inner pot into the Instant Pot before adding ingredients – this is a common mistake that all of us make at one point or another. Sometimes you're in a hurry and forget the inner pot isn't inside. To avoid this from happening, place a wooden spoon, a silicone mat, or glass lid on top of the pot when the inner pot isn't in. That way, you won't pour anything in by accident

- Overfilling the pot – if you realize too late that you overfilled the pot, don't worry, just allow for natural release. But, if you're worried about overfilling before you start cooking, remember your Instant Pot should be maximum 2/3 full, but for pressure cooking food that tends to expand during the cooking process, it should be ½ full maximum

- Using the timer button for cooking time – what most users don't know is that the timer button is intended for delayed cooking

- Not adding enough liquid – yet another common mistake, mainly among new users. Don't worry, your liquid adding skills will improve! Ideally, you should start with 1 cup of liquid until you are used to the unit. Adding the right amount of liquid is important because the appliance wouldn't be able to produce enough steam otherwise. Another thing to bear in mind is to add thickeners (when using them) only after the pressure cooking cycle

- Using rice button for preparing all types of rice – always keep in mind that different types of rice need different rice-to-water ratios and cooking times. In these cases, the manual button is more convenient

- Adding hot liquid in meals that require cold liquid – do you add hot water when a recipe specifically mentions cold water or some other type of liquid? Believe it or not, this is a common mistake. We usually add hot water because we want to speed things up, but it doesn't work like that. So, follow the recipe instructions religiously and add cold water or another type of liquid if the recipe requires it.

Now that you know what to do and mistakes to avoid, you are ready to start cooking. Let's go!

Chapter 5: Rise and Shine! Start Your Day with a Delicious Instant Pot Breakfast

Breakfast is the most important meal of the day and you should make it healthy. You have a long day ahead and your breakfast should boost your energy levels to keep you alert and productive.

Your breakfast should be high in vitamins, minerals, and other important nutrients that keep you healthy and full i.e. to prevent overeating.

Vegetarian or vegan breakfasts are highly versatile, they can include different ingredients so you can mix and match until you get the "winning" combination. This chapter leads you through breakfast ideas made with electric pressure cookers and an Instant Pot of course.

Breakfast quinoa

Servings: 6

Ingredients:

- Uncooked quinoa (rinsed) – 1½ cups

- Water – 2 ¼ cups

- Maple syrup – 2 tbsp.

- Vanilla – ½ tsp

- Cinnamon (ground) – ¼ tsp

- Salt – a pinch, according to your preferences

- Toppings: sliced almonds, fresh berries, coconut or almond milk

Instructions:

- The first step is to combine quinoa, water, vanilla, maple syrup, salt, and cinnamon in your pressure cooker

- Opt for 1 minute of cooking time at a high pressure

- When you hear the beep that turns your unit off, wait for about 10 minutes before you allow for Quick Release

- Remove the lid when the valve drops

- Fluff the cooked quinoa and serve with warm coconut milk and toppings of your choice

TIP: The recipe only suggests sliced almonds or berries, but you can add any topping you like.

Vegan quinoa burrito bowls

Servings: 4

Ingredients:

- Extra virgin olive oil – 1 tsp

- Red onion (diced) – ½

- Bell pepper (diced) – 1

- Salt – ½ tsp

- Cumin (ground) – 1 tsp

- Quinoa (rinsed) – 1 cup

- Salsa – 1 cup

- Water – 1 cup

- Black beans (cooked) – 1½ cup

- Toppings: guacamole, avocado, green onions, fresh cilantro, shredded lettuce, lime wedges

TIP: Instead of cooked black beans you can use 1 15-oz. can rinsed and drained, if it is more convenient to you. Also, you can use any type of topping you'd like, dare to be creative.

Instructions:

- Use the sauté feature to heat the oil in your Instant Pot, then proceed to add onion and pepper

- Sauté onion and pepper for about 5-8 minutes or until they soften and add salt, cumin

- Sauté for an additional minute

- Turn off the unit

- To ingredients in the Instant Pot, add salsa, quinoa, beans, and water and seal the lid

- Ensure that switch at the top is changed from *venting* to *sealing*

- Manually cook the ingredients for 12 minutes or choose the *rice* button

- Allow natural release

- Remove the lid, take the fork and fluff the cooked quinoa

- Serve with toppings of your choice

TIP: In case there are any leftovers, you can place them into an airtight container and store them in your fridge for up to a week.

Banana nut oatmeal

Servings: 3

Ingredients:

- Water – 3 cups
- Steel cut oats – 1 cup

- Bananas (sliced) – 2

- Cinnamon – 1 tsp

- Almonds (sliced) – ½ cup

- Maple syrup

Instructions:

- Put water, oats, one sliced banana, and cinnamon in the Instant Pot and stir

- Close your cooker properly and select *manual* option

- Set 3 minutes cooking time

- Once the cooking is over, allow for Natural Release

- After about 10 minutes open your cooker and take out cooked ingredients into a bowl

- Add remaining banana, maple syrup according to your liking, and sliced almonds

Brown rice congee with bok choy and shiitake

Servings: 4

Ingredients:

- Brown rice – ½ cup

- Mushroom broth – 2 cups

- Bok choy (chopped) – 2 cups

- Shiitake mushrooms (halved lengthwise) – 2 cups

- Ginger (fresh, minced) – 2 tbsp.

- Garlic (pressed or minced) – 2 cloves

- Warm water (if necessary) – 1 cup

- Tofu (cooked) – 1 block

- Soy sauce

TIP: If you can't find shiitake, use some other type of mushrooms instead.

Instructions:

- Add mushroom broth, brown rice, mushrooms, bok choy, ginger, and garlic in your Instant Pot or some other electric pressure cooker

- Press the *manual* button

- Set 40 minutes cooking time

- Allow Natural Release

- Scoop cooked ingredients into bowls and add scallions, soy sauce according to taste, and cooked tofu. You can top with anything you'd like

Tomato spinach quiche

Servings: 6

Ingredients:

- Vegan egg substitute – 24 oz.

- Non-dairy milk – ½ cup

- Salt – ½ tsp

- Pepper – ¼ tsp

- Baby spinach (chopped) – 3 cups

- Tomato (seeded, diced) – 3

- Green onions (sliced) - 4

- Tomato slices (for topping) – 4

- Shredded vegan cheese – ¼ cup

Instructions:

- Place a trivet into the cooker and add water (1½ cups)

- Take a large bowl and add egg substitute together with non-dairy milk, salt, and pepper. Start whisking

- Add tomato, spinach, green onions to a baking dish (1½ quart) and mix

- Pour egg mixture over the vegetables in the baking dish

33

- Stir

- Place tomato slices on top and sprinkle with shredded vegan cheese

- Gently place the baking dish onto the trivet

- Lock the lid

- Cook for 20 minutes at high pressure

- Allow Quick Release

- Broil until the quiche browns, if you want (not mandatory)

- Serve

Carrot cake oatmeal

Servings: 6

Ingredients:

- Vegan butter – 1 tbsp.
- Steel cut oats – 1 cup
- Water – 4 cups
- Carrots (grated) – 1 cup
- Maple syrup – 3 tbsp.
- Cinnamon – 2 tsp
- Pumpkin pie spice – 1 tsp
- Salt – ¼ tsp
- Raisins – ¾ cup
- Chia seeds – ¼ cup

Instructions:

- Start by adding butter to the cooker and then select *sauté* feature
- Once the butter melts, proceed to add oats and toast for 3 minutes while stirring constantly
- Add carrots, maple syrup, water, salt, pumpkin pie spice, and cinnamon to the pot
- Cook for 10 minutes at high pressure

- Allow the Natural Release

- Stir oats and add chia seeds and raisins

- Cover the cooked meal for about 10 minutes i.e. let it sit for a while until it reaches your preferred level of thickness

TIP: You can also add extra chia seeds and nuts along with maple syrup and non-dairy milk as toppings. This isn't mandatory, but a great variation to this lovely breakfast.

Apple cherry breakfast risotto

Servings: 1

Ingredients:

- Vegan butter – 2 tbsp.

- Arborio rice – 1½ cups

- Apples (diced, cored) – 2

- Cinnamon – 1½ tsp

- Salt – ¼ tsp

- Brown sugar – 1/3 cup

- Apple juice – 1 cup

- Non-dairy milk – 3 cups

- Cherries (dried) – ½ cup

TIP: For more servings, double or triple the amounts. You can also use smaller bowls to get more servings immediately.

Instructions:

- First, warm up the butter in your cooker for about 2-3 minutes

- When the butter melts, add rice and cook for 3-4 minutes (or until it is opaque) while stirring frequently

- Once the rice is ready, add spices and apples together with brown sugar

- Add non-dairy milk and apple juice

- Cook for 6 minutes and high pressure

- Allow Quick Release

- Remove the lid

- Add dried cherries to the mixture

- Pour the risotto into the bowl and sprinkle with sliced almonds, brown sugar, a splash of non-dairy milk, or add any other topping of your choice

- Serve

Vegan egg muffins

Servings: 4

Ingredients:

- Vegan egg substitute – 8 oz.

- Lemon pepper seasoning – ¼ tsp

- Vegan shredded cheese – 4 tbsp.

- Green onion (diced) – 1

- Vegan bacon (precooked, diced) – 4 slices

Instructions:

- Place the trivet into the cooker and add 1½ cups of water

- Add egg substitute and lemon pepper seasoning into the large bowl

- Beat thoroughly

- Divide Vegan bacon, Vegan cheese, and green onion between four muffin cups (make sure they are made of silicone), evenly

- Into each muffin cup, pour the egg mixture from the large bowl

- Using a fork stir carefully to combine ingredients into every muffin cup

- Place the cups onto the trivet

- Cover and lock the lid

- Cook for 8 minutes at high pressure

- Allow the Quick Release

- Serve immediately or store in the fridge

TIP: To reheat muffins, microwave for about 30 seconds. These delicious muffins can be stored up to a week in the fridge. You can prepare a weekly supply over Saturday and Sunday and have your breakfast ready throughout the week.

Pumpkin steel cut oats with pecan pie granola

Servings: 6

Ingredients for pumpkin steel cut oats:

- Vegan butter – 1 tbsp
- Steel cut oats – 1 cup
- Water – 3 cups
- Pumpkin puree – 1 cup
- Maple syrup – ¼ cup
- Cinnamon – 2 tsp
- Pumpkin pie spice – 1 tsp

- Salt – ¼ tsp

Instructions:

- Place the butter into the pot and select the *sauté* function

- Add oats when the butter melts and toast for about 3 minutes stirring consistently

- Proceed to add pumpkin puree, water, cinnamon, maple syrup, salt, and pumpkin pie spice into the cooker

- Cook for 10 minutes at high pressure

- Allow Natural release

- Carefully remove the lid when valve drops

- Give the oats a stir and let sit in an uncovered cooker for about 5 to 10 minutes or until they reach your desired thickness

- Serve oats together with a warm pecan pie granola, nondairy milk, and maple syrup

If you're wondering how to make a pecan pie granola, here is the simple recipe. P.S. You can bake it while you're cooking oats.

Ingredients for pecan pie granola:

- Old fashioned oats – 2 cups

- Salt – ¼ tsp

- Cinnamon – ¼ tsp

- Light brown sugar – ¼ cup

- Pecans (chopped) – ½ cup

- Coconut oil (or some other vegetable oil) – 2 tbsp.

- Maple syrup – ½ cup

- Vanilla extract – 1 tsp

Instructions:

- Start by preheating the oven to 350°F

- Set aside a cookie sheet with cooking spray or a parchment paper

- Take the medium sized bowl and combine salt, oats, pecans, and sugar

- Take the small bowl and add maple syrup, coconut oil (or some other vegetable oil), and vanilla extract. Stir in order to combine the liquid ingredients

- Proceed to pour liquid ingredients from the small bowl over dry ingredients in the medium sized bowl

- Stir thoroughly in order to mix and combine all ingredients. Make sure that pecans and oats are entirely covered

- Pour the mixture onto the cookie sheet and bake for about 25 minutes or until the pecan pie turns toasted brown

Chapter 6: Instant Pot Lunch Coming Right Up

Somehow it always seems all lunch ideas are locked somewhere and we can't think of anything to cook. How frustrating! In the end, we spend more time thinking about things to cook for lunch than actually preparing the meal. Let's put a stop to this daily frustration! This chapter brings you easy, simple, and nutritious vegetarian lunches you can make in your Instant Pot or any other electric pressure cooker. Excited? Here we go!

Baked sweet potatoes

Servings: 1

Ingredients:

- Sweet potato – 1
- Water (boiling) – 1 cup

TIP: For more servings, use more potatoes and increase the amount of water accordingly.

Instructions:

- Wash one (or more) sweet potato thoroughly. Using a fork, poke the potatoes two or three times

- Add 1 cup of hot or boiling water to the pot

- Place the trivet into the pot and make sure water level is below the level of the trivet

- Put sweet potato onto the trivet, making sure it is above the water level

- Cooking time depends on the size of the potato:
    o Small potatoes – 14 minutes
    o Medium potatoes – 16 minutes
    o Large potatoes – 18 minutes

- Choose the cooking time accordingly and cook at high pressure

- Allow the Natural Release

- As pressure in the cooker is decreasing, it is time to preheat the oven to 400°F

- Place the sweet potato onto a baking sheet

- Bake for 10-15 minutes

- Serve while it is still warm

- Sprinkle with herbs and salt or some other garnish, according to your liking

TIP: If you chose more than one sweet potato and they have different sizes, set the cooking time according to the largest potato in the bunch.

Shepherd's pie

Servings: 4 to 6

Ingredients for the filling:

- Onion (diced) – 1 cup

- Carrot (diced) – ½ cup

- Celery (diced) – 1/3 cup

- Turnip or sweet potato (diced, peeled) – ½ cup

- French green lentils (picked over, rinsed) – 1 cup

- Thyme (dried) – 1 tsp

- Bay leaf – 1

- Rosemary – ¼ tsp dried or ½ tsp fresh

- Vegetable stock – 1 ¾ cup

- Browned rice flour (or some other type of browned flour) – 1-2 tbsp.

- Vegan Worcestershire sauce – 1 tbsp.

- Tamari – to taste

- Tomatoes (fresh or canned) – 1 cup

- Tomato paste (optional) – 1 tbsp.

Ingredients for mashed potatoes:

- Potatoes – 4

- Vegetable stock – 1 cup

- Garlic (peeled, halved) – 6 cloves

- Soy or another nondairy milk – ½ cup

- Parsley (minced) – ½ cup

- Salt – to taste

- Vegan margarine (optional)

Instructions:

- Start by preparing mashed potatoes by adding diced potato into the pressure cooker together with garlic and vegetable stock. Cook at high pressure for 4 minutes and allow for the Quick Release. Proceed to mash the potato and add milk to achieve desired consistency. Add salt, parsley, and margarine (if using). Stir to combine thoroughly. Set aside

- Set your cooker to *sauté*

- Add celery, onion, and carrot and dry sauté the ingredients for about 3 minutes

- Proceed to add lentils, turnip or sweet potato, bay leaf, thyme, vegetable stock, and rosemary to the ingredients in your cooker

- Lock the lid and cook for 10 minutes at high pressure

- Allow the Natural Release

- Remove the lid

- Now it is time to add 1 tablespoon of browned flour along with Worcestershire sauce, tomato, tamari, and tomato paste (if you choose to use it)

- Stir the ingredients thoroughly

- Lock the lid and let the mixture in the pot sit for 3 minutes

- Allow the Quick Release the built-up pressure

- Remove the bay leaf

- Transfer the mixture to a casserole dish and top with mashed potatoes

- Run the dish under a broiler until mashed potatoes heat up or brown i.e. according to your liking

Spaghetti squash

Servings: 6

Ingredients:

- Dry black beans – 1 lb.

- Vegan bacon – 4 slices

- Onion (diced) – 1

- Garlic (minced or pressed) – 5-6 cloves

- Vegetable broth – 4 cups

- Water – 1 cup

- Kosher salt – 1 tbsp.

- Pepper – ½ tsp

- White rice (cooked) – for serving

Instructions:

- Start by placing black beans into the fine mesh strainer and before you proceed to the next step make sure you pick out shriveled beans and clean all the impurities

- Set the cooker to *sauté* option and cook Vegan bacon until it is crispy or turns lightly brown

- When the bacon is done, add onion and cook for 3-4 minutes while stirring frequently. Then, add garlic and cook for 30 additional seconds

- Add vegetable broth, beans, water as well as salt and pepper to the cooker

- Stir thoroughly

- Cook for 40 minutes on high pressure

- Allow the Natural Release

- Garnish with salt and pepper

- Pour the mixture as a topping over cooked rice

Spicy and sweet braised cabbage

Servings: 4

Ingredients:

- Sesame seed oil – 1 tbsp.

- Cabbage (divided into 8 wedges) – 1

- Carrot (grated) – 1

- Water – 1 ¼ cups+ 2 tsp

- Apple cider vinegar – ¼ cup

- Raw demerara sugar – 1 tsp

- Cayenne powder – ½ tsp

- Red pepper flakes – ½ tsp

- Cornstarch – 2 tsp

Instructions:

- Press the sauté feature and add the sesame seed oil

- Brown the cabbage wedges on one side only, it will take you about 3 minutes maximum

- Add 1 ¼ cups of water to the cooker as well as sugar, vinegar, red pepper flakes, cayenne powder, and stir

- Then, add cabbage wedges making sure browned side is facing up, and sprinkle grated carrots over the ingredients in your pot

- Cook for 5 minutes at high pressure

- Allow the Natural Release

- Place the wedges onto separate plates or on a serving platter

- Press the sauté again to reheat the cooking liquid

- Take a small bowl and combine 2 teaspoons of water along with cornstarch and pour the mixture into the pot where the cooking liquid is warming up

- Stir thoroughly to combine until it starts thickening

- Pour the sauce over cabbage

- Serve

Instant Pot biryani rice

Servings: 4

Ingredients:

- Red onion (diced) – ¼ cup
- Garlic (minced) – 1 clove
- Cumin seeds – 1 tsp
- Turmeric powder – ½ tsp
- Salt – ¼ tsp
- Cinnamon stick – 1
- Brown rice – 1 cup
- Water – 1 ½ cups
- Raisins – ¼ cup
- Mint (chopped) – ¼ cup
- Cashew (chopped, raw) – for garnish

Instructions:

- Start by soaking the rice in water for about 10 minutes
- Transfer soaked rice to a fine mesh strainer and rinse with tap water
- Set rice aside
- On your Instant Pot, press *sauté* feature and allow the cooker to heat up, it will take about 2 minutes
- Once the pot is warm, add onion together with cumin seeds, garlic, salt, turmeric, and cinnamon stick

- Sauté the ingredients for 1 minute and stir often to make sure nothing sticks to the bottom or sides of the cooker

- Turn off the pot

- Add rice and water, stir thoroughly

- Select the *multigrain* setting

- Set 25 minutes on timer

- When you hear the beep, allow for the Quick Release

- Uncover the pot and toss in mint and raisins, stir thoroughly

- While serving, garnish the meal with fresh mint leaves and chopped raw cashews

Lunch on-the-go – Vegan Instant Pot burgers

Servings: 8-10

Ingredients:

- Onion (minced) – 1 cup

- Ginger (fresh, grated) – 2 tsp

- Mushrooms (minced) – 1 cup

- Red lentils (picked over, rinsed) – 1 cup

- Sweet potatoes (peeled, cut into large pieces) – 1½

- Vegetable stock – 2 ¼ cups

- Hemp seeds – ¼ cup

- Parsley (fresh, chopped) – ¼ cup

- Cilantro (chopped) – ¼ cup

- Curry powder – 1 tbsp.

- Quick or baby oats – 1 cup

- Rice flour – 1-4 tbsp. (if necessary)

- Vegetable cooking spray (optional)

TIP: Choose mushrooms you like the most.

Instructions:

- Set your cooker to sauté

- Add ginger, onion, mushrooms and dry sauté the ingredients for 2-3 minutes

- Then, add sweet potato, vegetable stock, and red lentils into the cooker

- Cook for 6 minutes at high pressure

- Allow the Natural Release

- Transfer the mixture into a large bowl and let it cool off for about 15 minutes

- Preheat the oven to 375°F

- Take a baking sheet and line it with parchment paper and spray with cooking spray (if you want)

- Using a fork or a potato masher, start mashing the lentil mixture in the large bowl

- To the mashed lentils, add parsley, hemp seeds, curry powder, cilantro, and oats

- Ideally, the mixture should resemble a thick paste. If it's runny or doesn't have a paste-like consistency, add rice flour until you reach desired thickness. Add one tablespoon at the time so you don't go overdo it

- Start making patties, but make sure your hands are wet

- Place the patties onto the baking sheet

- Bake for 10 minutes per side or until they brown

- Wait for a few minutes for burgers to cool off before you serve

TIP: Leftover burgers can be stored in Ziploc bags and frozen for up to 3 months. You can also place them in the fridge and eat throughout the week.

Saffron quinoa with spring veggies

Servings: 4

Ingredients:

- Water (hot or warm) – ¼ cup
- Saffron threads – a pinch
- Quinoa (rinsed) – 1 cup
- Olive oil (optional) – 2 tsp
- Onion or leek (sliced) – 1 cup
- Garlic (minced) – 2 cloves

- Vegetable broth – 1½ cups

- Peas (sliced snow or sugar snap peas) – 1 cup or 12 medium-sized

  peas

- Asparagus (sliced) – 1 cup

- Lemon zest – 1-2 tsp

- Pine nuts (toasted, sliced) or slivered almonds – 2 tbsp.

- Fresh herbs (parsley, dill, or chives) – ¼ cup

- Lemon juice – a drizzle

- Vegan Parmesan cheese – for garnish

- Salt and pepper – to taste

Ingredients:

- First, place saffron into a bowl and pour in ¼ cup of water, let soak for 5 minutes

- Turn on the *sauté* feature and add olive oil, garlic, and onion or leek

- Sauté the ingredients for a few minutes

- Then, add quinoa and toast it

- Add saffron together with water it soaked in

- Stir thoroughly and add more water

- Cook for 5 minutes at high pressure

- Allow the Natural Release

- When the pressure drops, add peas and asparagus to the pot and cover the pot again for 2 minutes

- Add lemon zest, herbs, and nuts

- Serve

Sesame tofu

Servings: 4

Ingredients:

- Toasted sesame oil – 2 tsp
- Onion (sliced) – 2 cups
- Carrot (peeled, cut diagonally) – 1
- Sweet potato (peeled, diced) – 1 cup
- Garlic (minced) – 3 cloves
- Sesame seeds – 2 tbsp.
- Extra firm tofu (cubed) – 1 lb.
- Tamari – 1-2 tbsp.
- Rice vinegar – 1 tbsp.
- Vegetable stock – 1/3 cup
- Peas (sugar snap or snow, halved) – 2 cups
- Sriracha – 2 tbsp.
- Tahini (optional) – 2 tbsp.
- Scallions (chopped) – 2 tbsp.

Ingredients:

- Set your cooker to *sauté* and add the sesame oil

- Proceed to add carrot and onion together with sweet potato

- Sauté the added ingredients for 2 minutes

- Add garlic and one tablespoon of sesame seeds and sauté for another minute

- Then, add vegetable stock, vinegar, tamari, and tofu to the cooker

- Cook for 3 minutes at high pressure

- Allow Quick Release

- Add peas to the cooked ingredients and lock the pot again

- Cook for 1 minute at low pressure

- Allow Quick Release once again

- Add sriracha and tahini

- Garnish the mixture with remaining tablespoon of sesame seeds and chopped scallions

- Serve

Chickpeas minestrone

Servings: 4-6

Ingredients:

- Olive oil – 1 tbsp.

- Onion (chopped) – 1

- Carrot (chopped) – 1

- Celery stalk (chopped) – 1

- Garlic (minced) – 1 clove

- Rosemary – 1 sprig

- Sage – 1 sprig

- Bay leaf – 1

- Chickpeas (dry, quick-soaked or soaked) – 1 cup

- Water – 4 cups + 3 cups

- Tomato puree – 2 tbsp.

- Ditalini – 1 cup

- Salt and pepper – to taste

Instructions:

- Add olive oil to preheated cooker followed by onion, celery, and carrot. Stir frequently until they soften

- Add herbs and stir often for about 1 minute

- Add 4 cups of water along with tomato puree and chickpeas

- Lock the lid of pressure cooker

- Cook for 18 minutes at high pressure

- Allow the Natural Release

- Disengage the *keep warm* mode or unplug the pot and open the lid when the pressure indicator goes down

- Discard stems that remained from the herbs and remove the bay leaf

- Add 3 cups of water and seasonings (salt and pepper)

- Bring the ingredients to a boil and add pasta

- Cook for about 10 minutes (or according to pasta cooking instructions) without closing the lid

- Serve

Roasted potatoes

Servings: 3-4

Ingredients:

- Vegetable oil – 4-5 tbsp.

- Potatoes (baby or fingerling) – 1-2 lbs.

- Rosemary – 1 sprig

- Garlic (with outer skin on) – 3 cloves

- Vegetable stock – ½ cup

- Salt and pepper – according to your liking

Instructions:

- Preheat the pressure cooker and add vegetable oil

- When the oil is warm, add potatoes followed by rosemary and garlic

- Start rolling the potatoes around and brown them from all sides, it will take you about 8-10 minutes

- Using a knife, make a small cut in the middle of each potato

- Add vegetable stock

- Close the cooker

- Cook for 7 minutes at high pressure

- Allow the Natural Release

- Remove garlic cloves' skin

- Sprinkle potatoes with salt and pepper, or add some other seasoning or garnish and serve

Chapter 7: Instant Pot Dinners Even Omnivores Will Love

After a long day at work you are exhausted, but still in the mood to eat something delicious. While some people might think only unhealthy meals can be super delicious, the reality is different. Instant pot allows you to make a wide array of dinners without waiting for hours. This chapter brings you fast, simple, and easy vegetarian and vegan dinners that are so delicious even omnivores in your family will want to have a bite.

Instant Pot pasta with broccoli

Servings: 4

Ingredients:

- Whole wheat pasta of your choice – 1 16-oz. box

- Water – 4 cups

- Tomato basil sauce – 1 25-oz. jar

- Broccoli (frozen) – 1 bag

Instructions:

- Combine all ingredients in your Instant Pot

- Close and lock the lid

- Set pressure to low

- Press the *manual* button and use the arrow buttons to set 5 minutes

- Allow the Quick Release

- Let the ingredients in Instant pot cool off before serving

Yellow rice with peas and corn

Servings: 6-7

Ingredients:

- Basmati rice – 2 cups

- Olive oil – 3 tbsp.

- Onion (diced) – 1

- Salt and pepper – to taste

- Cilantro stalks (chopped, optional) – 3 tbsp.

- Garlic (diced) – 2 cloves

- Turmeric powder – 1 tsp

- Sweet corn kernels (frozen) – 1 cup

- Garden peas (frozen) – 1 cup

- Vegetable stock – 2 ¼ cups

Instructions:

- Take a large bowl and add rice together with cold water. Stir rice and drain

- Add more fresh water into the bowl and let it soak for about 30-45 minutes

- Using a sieve, drain the rice and rinse under cold tap water. Set aside

- Press the *sauté* feature on the Instant Pot and add olive oil together with onions and season with salt and pepper

- Stir frequently for 5 minutes or until onions soften

- To the pot, add garlic, turmeric, and cilantro followed by corn, rice, and peas

- Pour vegetable stock over the ingredients in your cooker

- Stir thoroughly and turn off the *sauté* feature

- Cover and lock the lid

- Cook for 4 minutes at high pressure

- Allow the Natural Release

- Open the lid and add a drizzle of olive oil

- Fluff the rice using a fork

- Serve

TIP: If you don't have enough time (or don't want) to soak rice, just rinse it thoroughly under cold tap water and add an additional minute to the total cooking time. Instead of 4, cook for 5 minutes.

Moroccan sweet potato and lentil stew

Servings: 3-4

Ingredients:

- Onion (diced) – 1
- Garlic (minced) – 3 cloves
- Sweet potato (peeled, cubed) – 1
- Carrots (peeled, diced) – 2
- Celery stalk (chopped) – 1
- Lentils (brown or green) – 1 cup
- Red lentils – ½ cup
- Vegetable broth – 2 cups
- Raisins – ¼ cup
- Tomatoes (diced) – 1 can
- Greens (diced, optional)
- Moroccan spice blend consisting of:
  - Turmeric – 1 tsp
  - Cinnamon – ½ tsp
  - Paprika – 1 tsp
  - Cumin – 1 tsp

- o Ginger – ¼ tsp
- o Coriander – 2 tsp
- o Chili flakes – a pinch
- o Cloves – a pinch
- o Black pepper – ½ tsp

Instructions:

- Turn on the *sauté* feature and add onions
- Sauté onions for 2-3 minutes while adding broth or water slightly so they don't stick to the bottom of your cooker
- Add garlic and sauté for an additional minute
- Add half of the spices from the Moroccan spices blend together with sweet potatoes, celery, carrots, and raisins
- Stir thoroughly and let cook for 1-2 minutes
- Add lentils and broth to the mixture
- Cover the Instant Pot and cook your dinner for 10 minutes at high pressure
- Allow the Natural Release
- Take off the lid and press *sauté* again
- Add tomatoes and the remaining half of Moroccan spices
- Cook for 5 minutes while stirring frequently
- Adjust the seasonings if necessary
- Turn off the Instant Pot and add greens before serving

TIP: Serve over quinoa for a delicious and filling dinner.

Spinach chana masala

Servings: 6-8

Ingredients:

- Chickpeas (raw) – 1 cup
- Cooking oil – 3 tbsp.
- Onions (chopped) – 1 cup

- Bay leaf – 1

- Garlic (grated) – 1 tbsp.

- Ginger (grated) – ½ tbsp..

- Water – 1 ½ cups

- Tomato puree (fresh) – 2 cups

- Roasted chickpea flour – 1 tbsp.

- Baby spinach (chopped) – 2 cups

- Salt and pepper – to taste

- Cilantro (fresh, chopped) – a fistful

- Lemon

Spices:

- Green chili (chopped) – 1

- Turmeric – ½ tsp

- Coriander powder – 1 tsp

- Chili powder – 2 tsp

- Cholay/chana masala – 1 tbsp.

Instructions:

- Place chickpeas into a mesh and wash them under cold tap water for 30 seconds

- Soak chickpeas overnight with 2 cups of water

- Drain excess fluid

- Turn on *sauté* feature on the Instant Pot and add a tablespoon of cooking oil after 3 minutes i.e. when the cooker warms up

- Add onions and sauté until translucent or about 2 minutes

- When onions are ready, it is time to add green chili, ginger, bay leaf, and garlic

- Cook the newly added ingredients for 20 seconds

- Then, add chana masala, chili powder, turmeric, coriander, and a tablespoon of water

- Sauté everything for 10 seconds before you add chickpea flour and then sauté for additional 10 seconds

- It's time to add fresh tomato puree, 1½ cups of water, and chickpeas

- Stir thoroughly

- Cover the Instant Pot and cook for 15 minutes at high pressure

- Allow the Natural Release

- Turn on the cooker to *sauté* mode again

- Add chopped spinach and season with salt and pepper

- Using a fork, mash a few chickpeas in order to get a thicker consistency

- Sauté for 3 minutes

- Turn off the cooker and add lemon juice and coriander

Crispy polenta bites

Servings: 4

Ingredients:

- Water or broth – 4 cups
- Coarse polenta – 1 cup
- Salt – to taste
- Fresh herbs (chopped) – ¼ cup
- Spices (of your choice) – 1-2 tsp

Instructions:

- Combine polenta, salt, and water in your Instant Pot along with seasonings
- Whisk thoroughly
- Cover the cooker and select *porridge*
- Adjust the cooker to 5 minutes
- Allow the Natural Release
- Let the mixture cool off while the oven is preheating at 450°F
- Prepare a baking sheet and line it with a parchment paper
- Scoop cooled off polenta out of the pot and place onto the baking dish
- Drizzle polenta bites with olive oil or cooking spray

- Bake dinner for 15-20 minutes

- Flip the polenta bites and bake for additional 15 minutes or until they turn golden in color

Steamed vegetables with garlic and parsley

Servings: 2

Ingredients:

- Carrots (peeled, sliced) – 2

- Brussels sprouts (halved) – 0.7lb.

- Water – 1 cup

- Salt and pepper – to taste

Ingredients for the butter sauce:

- Vegan butter – 1 oz.

- Baby capers – 1 tbsp.

- Parsley (fresh, chopped) – 1 tbsp.

- Garlic (diced) – 2 cloves

- Lemon peel – 1

- Lemon juice – 2 tbsp.

Instructions:

- Start by adding water to your pressure cooker

- Place the steam basket into the pot and arrange vegetables on it

- Sprinkle seasonings over vegetables

- Cook for 2 minutes at high pressure

- Allow the Natural Release

- When vegetables are cooking in the Instant Pot, take a small pot where you will combine all sauce ingredients except lemon juice

- Cook the sauce over medium-high heat for about 1 minute after the butter is melted stirring frequently

- Remove the sauce from your stove and set aside

- Take out the vegetables from the pot and transfer into a bowl where you'll drizzle them with lemon juice and add sauce

Thai red curry

Servings: 4-6

Ingredients:

- Onion (sliced) – 1 cup
- Garlic (minced) – 3 cloves
- Hot chili pepper – 1 tsp
- Split red lentils or chana dal – ½ cup
- Galangal slices (dried) – 2 pieces
- Kaffir lime leaves – 2
- Vegetable stock – 1 ¾ cups
- Coconut milk – ½ cup
- Thai red curry paste – 2 tsp
- Winter squash (peeled, cubed) – 4-5 cups
- Oyster mushrooms (sliced) – 4 oz.
- Broccoli florets – 1 cup
- Lime juice – 1-2 tbsp.
- Cilantro (chopped) – for garnish

Instructions:

- Set your cooker to *sauté*

- Add onion and sauté for 1 minute

- Add chili pepper and garlic and sauté for an additional minute

- Now it's time to add galangal, chana dal, ¾ cup of stock, lime leaves, curry paste, and coconut leaves

- Cook for 3 minutes at high pressure

- Allow the Natural Release

- Add mushrooms, squash, and remainder of stock

- Lock the lid and cook for 3 minutes at high pressure again

- Allow the Quick Release this time

- Add broccoli florets into the pot, cover and lock the lid, and let ingredients in the cooker stay for 2 minutes

- Remove the lid and discard galangal

- Transfer the mixture into a large bowl

- Sprinkle with cilantro and add lime juice and serve

Coconut cabbage

Servings: 4

Ingredients:

- Coconut oil – 1 tbsp.

- Brown onion (halved, sliced) – 1

- Salt – 1 + ½ tsp

- Garlic (diced) – 2 cloves

- Red chili (sliced) – ½

- Yellow mustard seeds – 1 tbsp.

- Mild curry powder – 1 tbsp.

- Turmeric powder – 1 tbsp.

- Cabbage (quartered, shredded) – 1

- Carrot (peeled, sliced) – 1

- Lemon or lime juice – 2 tbsp.

- Unsweetened coconut (desiccated) – ½ cup

- Olive oil – 1 tbsp.

- Water – 1/3 cup

TIP: If you can't find yellow mustard seeds, just opt for 1 teaspoon of mustard powder instead.

Instructions:

- Turn on your Instant Pot and select the *sauté* feature

- Add coconut oil together with onion and 1 teaspoon of salt

- Sauté the ingredients until they soften or about 3-4 minutes

- Then, add garlic, spices, and chili to the pot and stir thoroughly for 20-30 seconds

- It's time to add carrot, cabbage, coconut, lime juice, and olive oil

- Stir carefully, add water, and stir again

- Cover the Instant Pot and lock the lid

- Cook for 5 minutes at high pressure

- Allow the Natural Release

- Serve on its own or combine with some other dish

White bean stew

Servings: 6

Ingredients:

- Yellow-eye or navy beans (quick-soaked or soaked overnight) – 1 lb.

- Onion (chopped) – 1

- Garlic (minced) – 4 cloves

- Water – 5 cups

- Smoked paprika – 4 tsp (divided)

- Oregano (dried) – 2 tsp (divided)

- Cumin (ground) – 1½ tsp (divided)

- Basil (dried) – 1 tsp

- Winter squash or pumpkin (peeled, cubed) – 1 lb.

- Red bell pepper (chopped) – 1

- Jalapeno (seeded, chopped, optional) – 1

- Tomatoes (diced) – 1 15-oz. can

- Salt and pepper – to taste

- Kale (stems removed, sliced) – 1 bunch

- Corn (fresh or frozen, optional) – 1 cup

- Basil (fresh, chopped) – ½ cup

Instructions:

- Rinse the beans thoroughly after soaking them overnight (or a quick soak)

- Turn on the *sauté* feature on your Instant Pot and add onions together with a pinch of baking soda

- Sauté the onion until it starts to brown, add garlic, and sauté for 1 minute

- Add the beans together with water, 1 teaspoon of oregano, 2 teaspoons of paprika, 1 teaspoon of cumin, and dried basil

- Cover the pot and lock the lid

- Cook for 8 minutes at high pressure

- Allow a Quick Release

- Add squash, remaining seasonings, tomatoes, peppers, and lock the lid again

- Cook for 8 additional minutes at high pressure

- Allow a Natural Release this time

- Add corn and kale and let simmer until kale becomes tender or softer

- Add basil, stir, and let stay for 1 minute before you start serving

Mac and cheese

Servings: 6

Ingredients:

- Macaroni of your choice – 3 cups
- Water – 1 cup
- Vegetable broth – 2 cups
- Vegan butter – 2 tbsp.
- Sea salt and white pepper – to taste
- Ricotta-style vegan cheese – 1 cup
- Vegan cheddar cheese (shredded) – 2 cups

Instructions:

- In your Instant Pot, combine water, vegetable broth, macaroni, Vegan butter, and seasonings
- Cook for 6 minutes at high pressure
- Allow a Quick Release
- Add cheeses
- Stir thoroughly to combine macaroni and cheese
- Let dinner stand for 5-10 minutes before serving

Chapter 8: Instant Pot Soups

Everybody loves soups; they are healthy and easy on your stomach. The best thing about soups is their versatility, you can make them by combining a wide array of ingredients and they're ideal for every meal, regardless of the time of the day.

It doesn't have to take ages to make a delicious and healthy soup, with Instant Pot, you can do it fast and this chapter brings a few ideas that you can use.

Split pea soup

Servings: 4-6

Ingredients:

- Water – 5 cups
- Sweet potato (diced) – 1
- Split peas – 1 cup
- Navy beans (dried) – ½ cup
- Bay leaves – 3
- Liquid smoke – ½ tsp
- Nutritional yeast – to taste
- Salt and pepper – to taste

Instructions:

- Take your Instant Pot and add sweet potato, water, navy beans, split peas, bay leaves, and liquid smoke

- Cook for 20 minutes at high pressure

- Allow the Natural Release

- Add nutritional yeast, salt, and pepper

- Serve

Butternut squash soup

Servings: 4

Ingredients:

- Olive oil – 1 tsp

- Onion (chopped) – 1

- Garlic (minced) – 2 cloves

- Curry powder – 1 tbsp.

- Butternut squash (peeled, cubed) – 1 (3 lbs.)

- Sea salt – 1½ tsp

- Water – 3 cups

- Coconut milk – ½ cup

- Toppings: dried cranberries, hulled pumpkin seeds, or any other topping of your choice

Instructions:

- Press the *sauté* button on your Instant Pot

- Add olive oil and onion and sauté for 8 minutes or until it becomes tender

- Then, add garlic and curry powder, and sauté for 1 minute or until fragrant

- Turn off the cooker

- Add butternut squash together with water and salt

- Lock the lid

- Cook for 30 minutes at high pressure

- Allow the Natural Release

- Puree the soup in your cooker with an immersion blender

- Adjust seasonings

- Add toppings and serve

TIP: If it's inconvenient to you to puree the soup in the cooker, transfer it to another pot or a bowl.

Lentil and vegetable soup

Servings: 6+

Ingredients:

- Onions (diced) – 1 cup

- Potatoes (diced) – 6
- Carrots (sliced) – 3
- Broccoli (chopped) – 3 cups
- Lentils (dry) – 1 cup
- Water – 8 cups
- Salt and pepper – to taste
- Bay leaf – 1
- Onion powder – 1 tsp
- Garlic powder – 1 tsp
- Paprika – ½ tsp
- Thyme – ½ tsp

Instructions:

- Add all ingredients to your Instant Pot
- Cook for 15 minutes at high pressure
- Allow the Natural Release

Italian farmhouse vegetable soup

Servings: 4

Ingredients:

- Coconut oil – 1 tbsp.
- Brown onion (diced) – 1
- Salt – a pinch
- Red chili (sliced) – ½
- Celery sticks (sliced) – 2
- Button mushrooms (sliced) – 6
- Forest mushrooms (dried) – a handful

- Carrots (peeled, halved lengthwise) – 2

- Garlic (diced) – 4 cloves

- Kale leaves (sliced roughly, stems removed) – medium bunch

- Zucchini (diced) – 1

- Tomato passata or tinned chopped tomatoes – 1 cup

- Vegetable stock – 4 cups

- Bay leaf – 1

- Parsley (fresh, chopped) and lemon zest – for garnish

Instructions:

- Turn on the *sauté* feature on your Instant Pot

- Add coconut oil followed by salt, onion, carrots, celery, and stir thoroughly

- *Sauté* for 1-2 minutes

- Add zucchini, kale, tomatoes, bay leaf, and stock and stir once again

- Cook for 10 minutes at high pressure

- Allow the Natural Release

- Serve the soup in bowls and add lemon zest and chopped parsley as garnish

Zucchini basil soup

Servings: 2

Ingredients:

- Olive oil – 2 tsp
- Onion (chopped) – ¾ cup
- Garlic (chopped) – 4 cloves
- Zucchini (chopped) – 2
- Red chili flakes – 1 tsp
- Salt and pepper – to taste
- Water – 3 cups
- Basil (fresh, chopped) – ½ cup
- Greek-style Vegan yogurt – 2 tbsp.
- Vegan sour cream – 2 tbsp.
- Vegan Parmesan cheese (shredded) – 2 tbsp.

Instructions:

- Turn on *sauté* feature and add oil, onion, and garlic

- *Sauté* the ingredients until they soften

- Add salt and pepper, zucchini, red chili flakes, basil leaves, and water

- Close the Instant Pot and let it whistle for about 3-4 times

- Let the soup cool

- Open the pressure cooker again

- Blend ingredients with a blender until smooth

- Add more water if the mixture is too thick

- Heat the mixture again and add vegan sour cream and cheese

- Adjust the spices and serve

- You can add some lime juice to the soup as well

Beet soup

Servings: 4

Ingredients:

- White onion (chopped) – 1
- Salt and pepper – to taste
- White potatoes (peeled, diced) – 2
- Carrot (grated) – 1
- Beets (grated) – 2 medium or 3 small ones
- Garlic (diced) – 4 cloves
- Porcini mushrooms (dried) – 3-4 tsp
- Apple cider vinegar – 3 tbsp.
- Tomato paste – 1½ tbsp.
- Cabbage (sliced) – ¼ medium
- Vegetable stock – 1 cube
- Water – 5 cups
- Fresh parsley for serving
- Vegan-style sour cream

Instructions:

- Press sauté on your Instant pot and add olive oils with onions

- Sauté for 2 minutes or until onions soften

- Add carrots, potatoes, and beets into the pot

- Stir thoroughly

- Add cabbage, garlic, and remaining ingredients

- Cook for 10 minutes at high pressure

- Allow the Natural Release

- Sprinkle with parsley and cream before serving

Asparagus lemon soup

Servings: 4

Ingredients:

- Olive oil – 1 tsp

- White onion (chopped) – 1

- Garlic (chopped) 2 cloves

- Asparagus (trimmed) – 12 oz.

- Vegetable stock – 2 -2½ cups

- Mint flakes (dried) – ¼ tsp

- Lemon zest – ¼ tsp

- Lemon juice – 2 tsp

- Nutritional yeast – 1 tsp

- Salt and pepper to taste

TIP: If you ran out of vegetable stock you can use water instead.

Instructions:

- Take the trimmed asparagus and cut it into smaller pieces, then set it aside

- Turn on the *sauté* button and add oil, garlic, and onion

- *sauté* the ingredients for 2-3 minutes

- Add dried mint flakes, cut asparagus, lemon zest, and salt and pepper to the pot

- *Sauté* for a few minutes

- Add water or vegetable stock and stir

- Cover the cooker and lock the lid

- Cook for 3 minutes at high pressure

- Allow a Quick Release

- Uncover the pot and blend the ingredients using an immersion blender

- Add nutritional yeast and lemon zest

- Stir thoroughly

- Adjust the seasonings

- Garnish with asparagus tips and serve

Spicy carrot soup

Servings: 4-6

Ingredients:

- Carrots (peeled, chopped) – 8-10
- Onion (chopped) – 1
- Garlic (peeled) – 3 cloves
- Coconut milk – 1 14-oz. can
- Vegetable broth – 1½ cup
- Peanut butter – ¼ cup
- Red curry paste – 1 tbsp.
- Peanuts and cilantro – for toppings
- Salt and pepper – to taste

Instructions:

- Place all ingredients into the Instant Pot
- Cook for 15 minutes at high pressure
- Allow a Natural Release
- Let the mixture cool off for a few minutes
- Puree with an immersion blender until the mixture is smooth
- Season with salt and pepper

- Garnish with peanut and cilantro

- Serve

Chapter 9: It's Time for a Dessert

In the mood for something sweet? Believe it or not, you can use your Instant Pot to make super yummy desserts. Here are a few suggestions. You'll love them, for sure!

Pear and cranberry cake

Servings: 4-6

Ingredients (dry):

- Whole wheat pastry flour – 1¼ cup
- Cardamom (ground) – ½ tsp
- Baking soda – ½ tsp
- Baking powder – ½ tsp
- Salt – 1/8 tsp

Wet ingredients:

- Nondairy milk (unsweetened) – ½ cup
- Whole Earth Sweetener Agave 50 – ¼ cup
- Flaxseeds (ground) – 2 tbsp.
- Mild oil – 2 tbsp.

TIP: Make the cake oil-free by using applesauce instead of oil.

Mix-in ingredients:

- Pear (chopped) – 1 cup
- Cranberries (fresh, chopped) – ½ cup

You'll also need:

- Water – 1½ cups

Instructions:

- Take a 6 or 7-inch Bundt pan, oil it, and set it aside
- In a mixing bowl, combine all dry ingredients
- Combine all wet ingredients into a measuring cup
- Pour wet ingredients over dry ingredients in the bowl
- Add the mix-ins as well
- Place the Bundt pan into your cooker, with water in the bottom and steam rack
- Cover and lock the lid
- Cook for 35 minutes at high pressure
- Allow the Natural Release
- Let the cake cool off before you take it out of the pan or start serving
- You can also arrange it onto a serving platter and decorate with cranberries or other fruits

Instant Pot chocolate cake

Servings: 3

Ingredients:

- Green plantain – 1

- Banana (ripe) – ½

- Avocado (mashed) – ¼ cup

- Coconut oil (melted) – 2 tbsp.

- Honey – 2 tbsp.

- Carob powder – 5 tbsp.

- Apple cider vinegar – ½ tsp

- Baking soda – ¾ tsp

- Cream of tartar – 1/8 tsp

- Water – 1 cup

- Garnishes: coconut flakes, coconut cream, fruits, or other ingredients of your choice

Instructions:

- Blend plantain, banana, coconut oil, avocado, carob, honey, apple cider vinegar, cream of tartar, and baking soda in a food processor until you get a smooth mixture

- Grease 3 mini fluted pans with coconut oil

- Pour the batter from the food processor into the prepared pans

- Make sure each pan is about ¾ full

- Add water to your Instant Pot and place the trivet

- Place the pans onto the trivet

- Lock the lid and cook for 18 minutes at high pressure

- Allow the Quick Release

- Garnish your chocolate cake with fruit, coconut flakes, or coconut cream before serving

Chocolate pudding cake

Servings: 2-8

Ingredients:

- Semi-sweet chocolate morsels – 2/3 cup
- Egg substitute – ½ cup
- Applesauce – ½ cup
- Vanilla – 1 tsp
- Salt – a pinch
- Arrowroot – ¼ cup
- Cocoa powder – 3 tbsp.
- Powdered sugar – for topping

Instructions:

- Put trivet into the Instant Pot and add 2 cups of water
- Protect the chocolate morsels with heatproof ramekin and then place them onto the trivet
- Turn the cooker to *sauté* and melt the chocolate while the water is simmering underneath
- Once the chocolate is melted, remove ramekin
- Take a mixing bowl and combine applesauce, egg substitute, and vanilla

- Whisk thoroughly to blend all the ingredients

- Add dry ingredients to wet ingredients in the bowl

- Add melted chocolate

- Grease a 6-inch pan with oil and start dusting bottom and the sides of the cake pan with cocoa powder

- Pour the cake mixture onto the trivet

- Cook for 4 minutes at high pressure

- Allow the Quick Release

- Let the cake cool off for a few minutes before you transfer it from the cooker to a serving platter

- Decorate the cake with powdered sugar (optional)

Vanilla bean cheesecake

Servings: 8

Ingredients:

- Vegan cream cheese – 16 oz.

- Egg substitute – ½ cup

- Vanilla bean (scraped) – 1

- Vanilla extract – 1 tsp

- Sugar – ½ cup

- Raspberry chia jam – for topping

Instructions:

- Combine ingredients in a blender and blend until you get a smooth mixture

- Transfer the mixture into a 7-inch spring form pan

- Cover the pan with foil

- Place the pan into the Instant Pot and cook for 20 minutes at high or standard pressure

- Allow the Natural Release

- Let it cool off for about 30 minutes before you take out the cake and transfer it to the fridge

- Decorate it with jam or some other topping

Cashew lemon cheesecake

Servings: 8-12

Ingredients for crust:

- Quick oats – 1 cup
- Walnuts – ½ cup
- Dates (chopped, soaked in water for a few hours) – ½ cup

Ingredients for filling:

- Cashews (soaked in water for 2-4 hours) – 1 cup
- Coconut flour – ½ cup
- Coconut palm sugar – ¼ cup

- Vanilla nondairy milk – ½ cup
- Lemon zest (grated) – 1-2 tsp
- Lemon juice – 2 tbsp.
- Vanilla extract – 1 tsp
- Arrowroot powder – 1 tbsp.
- Strawberries, raspberries or other fruits (fresh) – for topping

Instructions:

- To your Instant Pot, add 1½ cups of water and place the steaming rack above the water level
- Start with the crust first; combine all ingredients in a food processor and blend. If the mixture seems too dry, add a tablespoon of date-soaking water. Transfer the mixture into a pan that you'll place in your cooker later
- Now, proceed to make the filling by adding cashews and half the soaking water to a blender and process until the mass is smooth. Then, add coconut flour, milk, palm sugar, lemon juice, lemon zest, and vanilla to cashews in food processor or blender. Add arrowroot now, and blend more
- Proceed to pour the filling mixture into the crust in the pan and cover with foil
- Place the pan into the pot
- Cook for 20 minutes at high pressure
- Allow the Natural Release

- Take out the pan and wait a while before you transfer the cake onto a serving platter

- Decorate with fruit

- Place the cake into the fridge

Baked apples

Servings: 6

Ingredients:

- Apples (cored) – 6

- Raisins – ¼ cup

- Red wine – 1 cup

- Raw demerara sugar – ½ cup

- Cinnamon powder – 1 tsp

Instructions:

- Place apples along the base of your Instant Pot

- Add raisins, red wine, cinnamon powder, and sugar to apples in the cooker

- Lock the lid and cook for 10 minutes at high pressure

- Allow the Natural Release

- Prepare six serving bowls and scoop an apple into each bowl along with a lot of sweet cooking sauce from the pot

Chapter 10: Miscellaneous – Other Instant Pot Meals to Make

This book provided a wide array of breakfast, lunch and dinner ideas, along with soups and desserts. However, your Instant Pot can do so much more. The final chapter mentions some useful recipes for other things you can make with your Instant Pot or some other electric pressure cooker.

Naan bread

Servings: 8

Ingredients:

- Plain flour – 1 cup

- Dry yeast – 1 tsp

- Sugar – ½ tsp

- Nondairy yogurt – 1 tbsp.

- Vegan butter – 1 tbsp.

- Salt – a pinch, to taste

Instructions:

- Take a small bowl where you will combine sugar, yeast, and 5 tablespoons of lukewarm water

- Cover the bowl and let it stay like that for 5-7 minutes

- In a deeper, larger bowl combine flour, the mixture from small bowl, nondairy yogurt, Vegan butter, and salt

- Knead the mixture to make a dough

- Make sure you have lukewarm water prepared and add tablespoon by tablespoon into the mixture in order to make the dough

- Cover the bowl with dough and let stay for 30 minutes

- Start kneading again for 1-2 minutes

- Divide dough into 8 smaller equal-sized balls

- Start rolling these small balls using plain flour so dough doesn't stick. Roll out the dough in an oblong of 5"

- Heat the electric pressure cooker but tilt it to the side

- Set a medium temperature and place rolled naan onto the "wall" of your cooker using hand mittens

- Cook until brown spots show up

- Remove from the cooker and brush the naan with melted Vegan butter

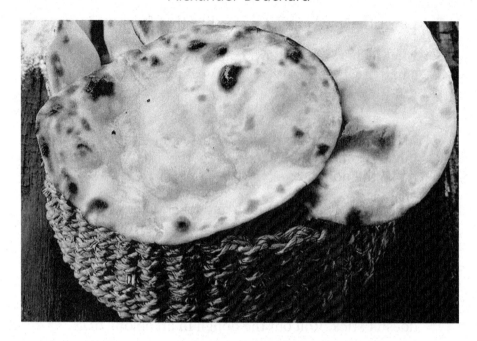

Corn on the cob with Cajun butter

Servings: 4-6

Ingredients:

- Cobs of fresh corn (peeled) – 6

- Water – 1 cup

- Vegan butter – 1.5 oz.

- Garlic (diced) – 1 clove

- Paprika powder – 1 + ½ tsp

- Onion powder – 1 + ½ tsp

- Cayenne powder – ½ tsp

- Oregano or thyme (dried) – 1 + ½ tsp

- Salt and pepper – to taste

- Lime (quartered) – 1

- Cilantro (fresh) – to serve

Instructions:

- Start by cutting corn in half and placing it in Instant Pot vertically (standing up)

- Add one cup of water

- Cook at high pressure for 2 minutes

- Allow the Quick Release

- Transfer the corn into a sieve

- Turn on *sauté* feature and add spices, garlic, and Vegan butter

- Stir the ingredients for 20-30 seconds and turn the heat off

- Take out the inner pot with spices mixture

- Transfer corn cobs back to the Instant Pot

- Pour the spices mixture over corn, cover, and shake to coat thoroughly

- Sprinkle with fresh cilantro and serve

Alexander Bouchard

Instant Pot hummus

Servings: 2 cups

Ingredients:

- Chickpeas or garbanzo beans (dried) – 1 cup

To soak:

- Salt – ½ tsp
- Water (hot) – 3-4 cups

To cook:

- Vegetable stock – 1 cube
- Water – 3 cups

Ingredients to make a dip:

- Olive oil – 2 tbsp.
- Light tahini – 3 tbsp.
- Lemon juice – ¼ cup + 2 tbsp.
- Garlic (chopped) – 2 cloves
- Salt – a pinch
- Cooking liquid – 2/3 cup
- Olive oil – for serving

Instructions:

- You can choose either to soak chickpeas or not. If you opt for soaking, then cover them with water for 8 hours

- If using dried chickpeas, add them to your instant pot along with 3 cups of water

- Add vegetable stock cube

- Cook for 35 minutes at high pressure

- Allow Natural Release

- Wait for the mixture to cool off before you scoop it into bowls

- Drizzle hummus with olive oil and a dash of cumin and paprika

TIP: You can also use homemade vegetable stock. Also, store hummus in an airtight container for up to 5-6 days.

Plant-based cheesy sauce

Servings: plenty for everyone at the table

Ingredients:

- Potato (peeled, chopped) – 2 cups
- Carrot (chopped) – 1 cup
- Yellow onion (chopped) – ½ cup
- Garlic (peeled) – 3 cloves
- Cashews (raw) – ½ cup
- Nutritional yeast – ½ cup
- Turmeric (chopped) – 1 tbsp. or 1 tsp of powder
- Salt and pepper – to taste
- Water – 2 cups

Instructions:

- Combine all above-mentioned ingredients in the Instant Pot
- Cook for 5 minutes at high pressure
- Allow the Quick Release
- Let the mixture cool off before you transfer it to the blender and puree until smooth and creamy, it will take about 2 minutes

Lentil Bolognese

Servings: 3-4

Ingredients:

- Beluga black lentils (washed) – 1 cup
- Fire roasted chopped tomatoes – 1-28.oz can
- Yellow onion (diced) – 1
- Garlic (minced) – 4 cloves
- Carrots (diced) – 3
- Tomato paste – 1 can
- Water – 4 cups

- Italian seasonings (dry) – 2 tbsp.

- Red pepper flakes, salt and pepper – to taste

- Balsamic vinegar

Instructions:

- Add all ingredients except vinegar to your Instant Pot

- Stir thoroughly to incorporate everything

- Cook for 15 minutes at high pressure

- Allow the Natural Release

- When you unlock the lid, add a drizzle of balsamic vinegar and stir again to combine

Conclusion

Thank you again for purchasing this book!

I hope this book was able to help you find useful vegetarian ideas for your Instant Pot.

Pressure cooking is becoming increasing popular nowadays and you should definitely take advantage of your Instant Pot or some other electric pressure cooker.

Throughout this book, you have had the opportunity to learn more about Instant Pot and pressure cooking. Most importantly, the book deliver a multitude of ideas that you can use to make your meals from breakfast to desserts.

The next step is to determine what meal you're going to make now and start cooking. These recipes also encourage you to mix and match ingredients, experiment, and explore your creativity in the kitchen.

There is no need to wait, start today!

Thank you and good luck!

CPSIA information can be obtained
at www.ICGtesting.com
Printed in the USA
LVOW13s2141090518
576659LV00033B/585/P